Winter Is Here!

By Jane Belk Moncure

Illustrated by Frances Hook

THE CHILD'S WORLD

ELGIN, ILLINOIS 60120

Library of Congress Cataloging in Publication Data

Moncure, Jane Belk.
  Winter Is Here!

  SUMMARY: Describes in verse the sights, sounds, and
activities of winter.
  [1. Winter—Fiction. 2. Stories in rhyme]
I. Hook, Frances. II. Title.
PZ8.3.M72Wi   [E]   75-14201
ISBN 0-913778-10-9

PICTURE
WORDS

ice on
a pond

a ball
of holly,
pine and
spice

icicles

candles

a snowflake

birds

a tiny gingerbread cookie tree

a snowball
and mittens

a snowman

A snowy day.

A blowy day.

Play with me on a snowy day.

My dog is ready to run and play.

I am ready, too.

Are you?

Snowman, snowman, round and fat.

Do you need two ears?

Do you need a hat?

You have two eyes and a

   carrot nose.

Could you feel winter if you

   had toes?

Do birds like winter?

Do birds like snow?

Do birds feel icy winds that blow?

One bird sits; one bird hops.

One bird calls, "Dee-dee-dee."

Is he calling, "Please feed me"?

Can you hear winter sounds?

Can you touch winter snow?

Can you smell winter smells as the
candles glow?

Look in the window. What do you see?

A tiny gingerbread cookie tree! A ball
of holly, pine, and spice!

Winter smells are very nice.

Do you like winter?
Do you like ice?
I think icicles are very nice.
I see ice on the pond, ice on
the tree, ice on my mittens,
and ice on me.

I slip and slide on the slippery ice.

Ice on the pond is very nice.

Where are the fish?

Are they under the ice?

Do fish think winter is very nice?

I can be an icicle in the snow.

Around and around and around I go.

I can be a snowflake.
Down I go into a soft white
bed of snow.

I can be a snowbird.
Up I fly.
Up, up, up
into the sky.

I can be a snowball.
I roll away,
 away down the hill
 on a snowy day.

Winter is here.
Will winter stay?
Will my snowman stay
    for another day?
When will winter melt away?

Winter